COPYCAT RECIPES

The Complete Step-By-Step Cookbook Whit 50 Recipes.
Learn To Cook From The Globally Famous Restaurant And Enjoy
Delicious Meals At Home

Belinda McDaniel

Table of Contents

—

Introduction

Copycat recipes are continually being tested to ensure that you create the restaurant's exact dishes. Expert chefs spend hours tailoring these recipes to get the perfect flavor. Such recipes are as close to the real thing as being in your kitchen right at your favorite restaurant. How will you save money on these copycat recipes?

With these recipes, the amount of money you'll save will be shocking. Imagine spending a night out at your favorite restaurant, for you and your significant other. You get an appetizer, two begins, and a dessert is shared. You spent between $55 and $70 comfortably with beverages, food, and a tip. You will probably spend about a third of that on producing these same recipes at home without losing any taste. So, you could use the copycat recipes to prepare three different meals at home for what it would cost you to eat out once. So, where are these recipes you looking at?

That's the copycat recipe's great thing. You won't need any special cooking appliances or any unique ingredients. If you do any cooking, you probably already have the things you need around your kitchen. Whatever you don't have should be readily available at your local food mart. There's nothing exotic about this.

Think back to the last time you've been to your favorite restaurant. Was there a line? When seated, how did you anxiously wait for your favorite meal to arrive? Then that feeling came when the waitress put it on the table. Finally, ah, was it perfect? Or was it not? Like it just wasn't cooked right. Or maybe it wasn't warm enough, or they left a topping out? What did you feel when you got this bill? Did 'Aahhh' become 'woooah'? I'll show you how you can stop such problems associated with eating out. It's all by using reliable and proven copycat recipes. Want to know the top five reasons to make your favorite home-made foods?

Cost: How much do copycat recipes save you? Let's say you're out to eat with your significant other. Now let's add some drinks and a tip. You have invested $60-$80 comfortably anywhere in the neighborhood. You get an appetizer, two exits, and perhaps a dessert is split. You might have made the same meal at home for $25-$30, less than half the eating out the price! And in the meantime, don't lose any flavor. That is a considerable saving in these economic times. That sounds great, but we are talking about how many recipes?

Health: That's the beautiful thing about making home copycat recipes. Whether to provide a different flavor to the food, or add your homegrown vegetables.

Quality: A team of professional chefs created these recipes. We have checked over and over to make sure you get the exact ingredients and correct steps to make your favorite dish. Of course, you can go online to find recipes that claim to be copycats of popular restaurants. Yes, it's free. And it's a reason they're free. These are not real recipes for copycat purposes. They are not even close. I've tried a couple, and to be honest; they weren't close; they weren't also good. I'll show you how to get the real copycat recipes and get your freedom back.

Freedom: Will you know how much you waste eating out of your time and freedom? Can you get the midnight meal you prefer? When watching your favorite series, will you eat your favorite meal? For instance, you are driving to the restaurant, waiting to sit down, waiting to get your appetizer, waiting to get your feed, waiting to get your dessert and, you guessed it, waiting to pay your bill. So, how much did you expect? Two hours, three more hours? Take your time and freedom back and fix your favorite meals at home. Use these copycat recipes when you want to make your favorite meal and how you want it.

All of these dishes are custom-tested and customer-approved restaurants. Do you have an enjoyable meal at a restaurant and would like to replicate it at home? There are a few cloned restaurant recipes now because some of you have been asking for them. Almost every one of us went to a restaurant and had a meal that was so delicious that we wanted to know how to make that meal at home. There is a staggering increase in interest in discovering online restaurants.

Cooking also shows that there is no shortcut to performance. Now, I will create my meals and present them whenever I cook. Getting into the habit of eating at home is hard, but learning how to prepare your favorite restaurant meals in the comfort of your kitchen can make it a little easier. It's not that hard to learn how to cook secret restaurant meals. People think you need a background in cooking or a degree in culinary arts to be able to cook those secret dishes. What better way to control the consistency of what you and your family shove into your mouth than by preparing your meals? Today, this remains the best reason to learn to cook: because you can.

Tomato Basil Soup

Preparation time: 10 minutes
Cooking time: 20 minutes
Serving: 8
Ingredients:

- 3 tablespoons olive oil
- 1 small garlic clove, finely chopped
- 1 10 ¾-ounce can condensed tomato soup
- ¼ cup bottled marinara sauce
- 5 ounces of water
- 1 teaspoon fresh oregano, diced
- ½ teaspoon ground black pepper
- 1 tablespoon fresh basil, diced
- 6 Italian-style seasoned croutons
- 2 tablespoons Parmesan cheese, shredded

Directions:
Heat oil in a pan over medium heat. Add garlic and stir fry for 2 to 3 minutes or until garlic is soft and aromatic.
Pour tomato soup and marinara sauce into pan and stir. Add water gradually. Toss in oregano and pepper. Once simmering, reduce heat to low. Cook for about 15 more minutes until all the flavors are combined. Add basil and stir.
Transfer to bowls. Add croutons on top and sprinkle with Parmesan cheese.
Serve.
Nutrition: Calories 1874 kcal Protein: 34.39 g Fat: 80.69 g Carbohydrates: 254.38 g

Chevy's Chipotle Slaw

Preparation time: 10 minutes
Cooking time: minutes
Serving: 6
Ingredients:

- 3 cups finely shredded white cabbage
- 3 cups finely shredded red cabbage
- ¾ cup Sweet Chipotle Dressing
- Sweet Chipotle Dressing
- 1 tablespoon diced onion
- 2 teaspoons minced garlic
- 1 chipotle pepper in adobo sauce, diced
- 1 tablespoon adobo sauce
- 2 tablespoons mustard
- ½ teaspoon ground cumin
- ½ cup diced fresh tomatoes
- 2 tablespoons chopped cilantro
- ⅔ cup of seasoned rice wine vinegar
- ¼ teaspoon black pepper
- 1 teaspoon salt
- 2 tablespoons honey
- ½ cup olive oil

Directions:
Shred the cabbage and toss it in a large bowl.
In a blender or food processor, combine all the dressing ingredients
EXCEPT the oil until smooth.
While the blender is running, drizzle in the oil to make an emulsion.
Pour ¾ cup of the dressing over the cabbage and toss to coat.
Store the remaining dressing in an airtight container in the fridge for up
to 1 week.
Nutrition: Calories 1449 kcal Protein: 18.59 g Fat: 116.68 g
Carbohydrates: 91.74 g

Café Rio's Black Beans

Preparation time: 10 minutes
Cooking time: 30 minutes
Serving: 8
Ingredients:

- 2 tablespoons olive oil
- 3 cloves garlic, minced
- 1 jalapeño pepper, minced
- 2 (15-ounce) cans black beans (one can drain, one with liquid)
- 2 teaspoons cumin
- 12 ounces tomato juice
- 1 teaspoon salt
- ½ teaspoon black pepper
- ¼ cup chopped cilantro

Directions:
In a large non-stick skillet over medium heat, warm the oil and sauté the garlic and jalapeño until fragrant.
Add the beans and cumin. Bring the mixture to a simmer and cook for 5–10 minutes, until some of the liquid has evaporated.
Stir in the tomato juice, salt, pepper, and cilantro.
. Cook to heat through, and serve.
Nutrition: Calories 703 kcal Protein: 27.72 g Fat: 36.8 Carbohydrates: 78.88 g

Applebee's Cheese Chicken Tortilla Soup

Preparation time: 10 minutes
Cooking time: 40 minutes
Serving: 6-8
Ingredients:

- 2 tablespoons vegetable oil
- 2 teaspoons minced garlic
- 1 medium chopped onion
- ¼ cup chopped green pepper
- 1 (15 ounces) can tomato purée
- 4 cups chicken stock
- 1 teaspoon sugar
- ½ teaspoon salt
- 1 teaspoon chili powder
- 1 teaspoon Worcestershire sauce
- 10 (6") yellow corn tortillas
- 4 tablespoons flour
- ½ cup of water
- 1-pound cooked chicken
- 1 cup cream
- ¼ cup nonfat sour cream

- 8 ounces Velveeta cheese, cut into 1" cubes

Directions:
In a large stockpot over medium heat, add oil and sauté garlic, onions, and green peppers.
Add chicken stock, tomato purée, sugar, salt, chili powder, and Worcestershire sauce to the pot.
Bring to a boil, then reduce heat and simmer for 20 minutes.
Cut tortillas into ¼ " strips and bake in the oven at 400°F for 6–8 minutes until crispy.
In a small bowl, mix flour and water, then whisk into the soup.
Add chicken and cream, bring to a boil, then simmer for 5 minutes.
Ladle into bowls and garnish with the sour cream, cheese, and tortilla strips.
Nutrition: Calories 8008 kcal Protein: 926.91 g Fat: 416.64 g Carbohydrates: 86.1 g

California Pizza Kitchen Pea and Barley Soup

Preparation time: 10 minutes
Cooking time: 2 hours and 20 minutes
Serving: 8
Ingredients:

- 2 cups split peas
- 6 cups of water
- 4 cups chicken broth
- 1/3 cup minced onion
- 1 large clove minced garlic
- 2 teaspoons lemon juice
- 1 teaspoon salt
- 1 teaspoon granulated sugar
- ¼ teaspoon dried parsley
- ¼ teaspoon white pepper
- Dash dried thyme
- ½ cup barley
- 6 cups of water
- 2 medium diced carrots
- ½ stalk diced celery

Directions:

Rinse and drain the split peas and add them to a large pot with 6 cups of water, chicken broth, onion, garlic, lemon juice, salt, sugar, parsley, pepper, and thyme. Bring to a boil. Reduce heat and simmer for 75 minutes, or until the peas are soft.

While the peas are cooking, combine the barley with 6 cups of water in a saucepan. Bring to a boil, reduce heat, and simmer for 75 minutes, or until the barley is soft and most of the water has been absorbed.

Drain the barley in a colander and add it to the split peas. Add the carrots and celery and continue to simmer the soup for 15–30 minutes, or until the carrots are tender. Stir occasionally.

Turn off the heat, cover the soup, and let it sit for 10–15 minutes before serving.

Nutrition: Calories 3423 kcal Protein: 319.53 g Fat: 78.61 g Carbohydrates: 356.35 g

Greek Lemon Chicken Orzo Soup Slow-Cooked: Panera Copycat

Preparation time: 20 minutes
Cooking time: 1 hour
Serving: 4-12
Ingredients:

- 2 tbsp. Olive oil
- 2 lb. into ½-inch pieces Chicken breasts
- 5 - 14.5 oz. each Reduced-sodium chicken broth
- 8 cups freshly chopped kale/spinach/Swiss chard
- 2 large Carrots
- 1 small Onion
- 4 tsp. /1 medium lemon Lemon zest
- .25 cup Lemon juice
- .5 tsp. Black pepper
- 4 cups Cooked brown rice

Directions:

Remove all of the bones and skin from the chicken breasts. Coarsely chop the kale. Finely chop the onion and carrots. Cut and slice the lemon in half and then into wedges.

Heat one tablespoon of oil in a skillet using the med-high temperature setting.

Add half of the breasts of chicken into the skillet and fry it until it's browned. Transfer the chicken to a six-quart slow cooker.

Finish cooking the chicken and toss it in with the veggies, lemon juice, lemon zest, broth, and pepper.

Prepare the chicken covered with the top using the low setting until the chicken is tender (four to five hours). Stir in the rice, heating thoroughly and serve.

Nutrition: Calories 2852 kcal Protein: 168.59 g Fat: 153.31 g Carbohydrates: 212.14 g

Chili: Wendy's Copycat

Preparation time: 15 minutes
Cooking time: 1 hour and 15 minutes
Serving: 6
Ingredients:

- 2 tbsp. Olive oil
- 1 Medium onion
- 2 stalks Celery
- 1 medium green bell pepper
- 1 tbsp. Tomato paste
- 1.5 lb. Ground beef
- 3 tbsp. Chili powder
- 2 tsp. Ground cumin
- 1 tsp. Garlic powder
- Black pepper & kosher salt (as desired)
- 28-oz. can Crushed tomatoes
- 15-oz. can of each Kidney & Pinto bean

Note: Reserve the juices in the beans.
For Serving:
1. Shredded cheddar
2. Sliced green onions

Directions:
Use the medium temperature setting to warm a skillet with the oil.
Mince/chop and sauté the onions, celery, and bell peppers (5 min.).
Stir in the tomato paste and stir (2 min.) and add the beef to simmer another six minutes. Drain the fat and place the meat back on the burner.
Add in the chili powder, pepper, salt, garlic powder, and cumin.
Pour in the tomatoes, plus half a can of water, to remove the remainder of the juices. Add the beans and liquids.
Stir well and wait for it to boil. Once boiling, set the temperature on low and simmer for an additional 40 minutes.
Adjust seasonings as desired and serve with fresh onions and cheddar as desired.
Nutrition: Calories 3164 kcal Protein: 269.58 g Fat: 158.18 g Carbohydrates: 169.43 g

Olive Garden Roasted Butternut Squash

Preparation time: 10 min
Cooking time: 1 hour
Serving: 6
Ingredients:

- 8 cups Butternut squash
- 1 teaspoon Salt
- 1 cup Sweet white wine (riesling works well)
- 2 tablespoons Vegetable oil

Directions:
Heat your oven to 400 degrees F. Spray a 9-by13-inch baking dish with cooking spray.
Toss the butternut squash, salt, and oil in a bowl. Spread the mixture on a rimmed baking sheet and place in the oven to bake for approx. 30 minutes.
Move the squash pieces to the prepared baking dish, pour the wine over the squash, and then place it in the oven to bake for about 20 more minutes, until the squash is tender. Smaller squash pieces will take a shorter time to cook.
Serve immediately.
Nutrition: Calories 959 kcal Protein: 22.56 g Fat: 36.2 g
Carbohydrates: 160.22 g

Compilation of Famous Main Dishes

Panda Express's Beijing Beef

Preparation time: 20 minutes
Cooking time: 15 minutes
Serving: 4
Ingredients:
1-pound flank steak
1 cup canola oil
4 cloves garlic, minced
1 yellow onion, sliced
1 red bell pepper, cut into 1-inch strips
2 tablespoons + 1 teaspoon cornstarch, divided
¼ teaspoon salt
3 egg whites, beaten
½ cup of water
¼ cup of sugar
3 tablespoons ketchup
6 tablespoons hoisin sauce

1 tablespoon soy sauce
2 teaspoons oyster sauce
4 teaspoons sweet chili sauce
1 teaspoon crushed red peppers
2 tablespoons apple cider vinegar

Directions:
Cut the flank steak against the grain into ¼-inch slices. Place the beef, egg, salt, and 1 teaspoon of cornstarch in a mixing bowl. Cover and refrigerate for at least an hour. In another mixing bowl, whisk together the water, sugar, ketchup, hoisin sauce, soy sauce, oyster sauce, chili sauce, crushed red pepper, and apple cider vinegar. Remove the beef from the refrigerator and place it in a separate dish. Discard the remaining marinade. Sprinkle the beef with 2 tablespoons of cornstarch and stir. Shake off any excess cornstarch. In a medium saucepan, heat the oil over medium-high heat. When hot, fry the beef in batches, about 2–3 minutes. Remove from oil and set on a paper-towel-lined plate to drain. To a large skillet, add 2 tablespoons of the same oil you fried the beef in. Heat over medium-high heat. When hot, add the onion and pepper and cook for about 3 minutes. Add the garlic and cook about 30 seconds more, then remove from the skillet and add to the plate with the beef. Add the sauce you prepared earlier to the skillet and cook over high heat until it thickens. Add the beef and vegetables, stirring to coat.

Nutrition: Calories 3181 kcal Protein: 121.62 g Fat: 253.47 g Carbohydrates: 104.98 g

Panda Express's Copycat Beef and Broccoli

Preparation time: 30 minutes
Cooking time: 15 minutes
Serving: 4
Ingredients:
2 tablespoons cornstarch, divided
3 tablespoons Chinese rice wine, divided
1 pound flank steak, cut thinly against the grain
1 pound broccoli florets, chopped into small pieces
2 tablespoons oyster sauce
2 tablespoons water
1 tablespoon brown sugar
1 tablespoon soy sauce
1 tablespoon cornstarch
2 tablespoons canola oil
¼ teaspoon sesame oil
1 teaspoon ginger, finely chopped
2 cloves garlic, finely chopped
2 teaspoons sesame seeds
Directions:
In a large Ziploc bag, add 1 tablespoon cornstarch and 2 tablespoons
Chinese rice wine. Place beef inside and seal tightly. Massage bag to
fully coat beef. Set aside to marinate for at least 20 minutes.
Rinse broccoli and place in a nonreactive bowl. Place a wet paper towel
on top, then microwave for 2 minutes. Set aside.

Stir oyster sauce, water, 1 tablespoon Chinese rice wine, brown sugar, soy sauce, and remaining cornstarch in a bowl until well mixed. Set aside.

Heat wok over high heat. You want the wok to be very hot. Then, heat canola and sesame oil in wok and wait to become hot.

Working in batches, add steak, and cook over high heat for 1 minute. Flip, and cook the other side for another 1 minute. Transfer to a plate. To the same wok, add garlic and ginger. Sauté for about 10 to 15 seconds then return beef to wok. Toss in cooked broccoli. Slightly stir the prepared sauce to make sure cornstarch is not settled on the bottom, then add to wok. Toss everything in the sauce to combine. Continue cooking until sauce becomes thick.

Garnish with sesame seeds. Serve.

Nutrition: Calories 1292 kcal Protein: 121.19 g Fat: 66.4 g Carbohydrates: 53.68

PF Chang's Mongolian Beef

Preparation time: 15 minutes
Cooking time: 10 minutes
Serving: 4-6
Ingredients:
1 cup of vegetable oil
1½ pounds flank steak
½ cup cornstarch
¼ teaspoon red pepper flakes (optional)
One bunch green onion, diagonal cut into 2-inch pieces
Rice for serving
Sauce
1 tablespoon vegetable oil
1–2 teaspoons ginger, minced
1 tablespoon garlic, minced
½ cup of soy sauce
½ cup of water
¾ cup dark brown sugar
Directions:
Prepare the sauce by heating the oil in a medium saucepan over medium-high heat. Add the ginger and garlic. Stir and cook for about 30 seconds.

Add the soy sauce, water, and brown sugar. Bring mixture to a boil, then reduce heat slightly and allow to simmer until the sauce begins to thicken.

Prepare steak by slicing it into ¼-inch slices, working against the grain to keep it tender. Place the cornstarch in a shallow dish, then dredge the sliced beef in the cornstarch to coat, shaking off any excess.

While the beef sits, heat the oil in a skillet over medium-high heat. When hot, add the beef and cook for about 3 minutes or until brown and crisp. Make sure to cook on both sides.

Remove the beef from the skillet and place on a plate. Drain the oil from the skillet and put the beef back in. Add the sauce and cook, stirring to make sure the beef is covered with sauce.

Sprinkle in the red pepper flakes and green onions.

Remove from heat and serve with rice.

Nutrition: Calories 4212 kcal Protein: 167.65 g Fat: 295.68 g Carbohydrates: 221.92 g

PF Chang's Beef A La Sichuan

Preparation time: 20 minutes
Cooking time: 10 minutes
Serving: 4-6
Ingredients:

- Stir-fry
- 1-pound flank steak or sirloin, sliced thin
- 4 medium celery ribs
- 2 medium carrots
- 1 green onion
- ¼ cup peanut oil or canola oil
- ¼ cup cornstarch
- ½ teaspoon red pepper flakes
- 1½ teaspoons sesame oil
- Sauce
- 3 tablespoons soy sauce
- 2 tablespoons hoisin sauce
- 1 tablespoon garlic and red chili paste
- ½ teaspoon Chinese hot mustard
- One teaspoon rice wine vinegar
- ½ teaspoon chili oil

- 2 teaspoons brown sugar
- 1 teaspoon garlic, minced
- ½ teaspoon fresh ginger, minced
- ½ teaspoon red pepper flakes

Directions:
Whisk together all of the sauce ingredients in a mixing bowl. Set aside. Slice the carrots and celery as thinly as possible and set aside. Place the sliced beef in a medium bowl and sprinkle it with the cornstarch. Make sure every piece is coated. Allow sitting for 10 minutes. Heat the oil in a large skillet or wok over medium-high heat and cook the beef until crispy, about 4–5 minutes. When done, remove beef from the oil to a paper-towel-lined plate to drain. Discard any oil remaining in the skillet. Add the sesame oil to the same skillet and heat over high heat. Add the celery, stir, and cook for about 1 minute. Add the crushed red pepper and stir. Add the carrots, cooking and stirring for another 30 seconds. Add the beef and green onions and stir, then pour the sauce into the skillet and bring to a boil. Allow to cook for one more minute, then serve over rice.
Nutrition: Calories 1730 kcal Protein: 112.13 g Fat: 102.9 g Carbohydrates: 84.99 g

Southwest Steak

Preparation time: 20 minutes
Cooking time: 10 minutes
Serving: 2
Ingredients:

- 2 (6-ounce) sirloin steaks, or your favorite cut
- 2 teaspoons blackened steak seasoning
- ½ cup red peppers, sliced
- ½ cup green peppers, sliced
- 2 tablespoons unsalted butter
- 1 cup yellow onion, sliced
- 2 cloves garlic, minced
- Salt, to taste
- Pepper, to taste
- 2 slices cheddar cheese
- 2 slices Monterey jack cheese
- Vegetable medley or/and garlic mashed potatoes, for serving.

Directions:
Preheat a cast-iron (or other heavy skillets) or a grill.
Season the meat with steak seasoning and cook to your desired doneness (about 3–4 minutes on each side for medium-rare).

In another skillet, melt the butter and cook the peppers, onion, and garlic. Season with salt and pepper.

Before the steak has reached your desired doneness, top with a slice of each cheese and cook a bit longer until it melts.

Serve the steaks with pepper and onion mix and garlic mashed potatoes.

Nutrition: Calories 627 kcal Protein: 24.31 g Fat: 49.52 g Carbohydrates: 21.71 g

Chicken Fingers

Preparation time: 20 minutes
Cooking time: 10minutes
Serving: 6
Ingredients:

- 6 boneless skinless chicken breasts, cut into strips
- 1 egg, beaten
- 1 cup buttermilk
- 1 ½ teaspoon garlic powder
- 1 cup all-purpose flour
- 1 cup seasoned bread crumbs
- 1 teaspoon salt
- 1 teaspoon baking powder
- 1 quart oil, for frying
- Honey Mustard Sauce
- ¼ cup mayonnaise
- ¼ cup Dijon mustard
- ¼ cup honey
- 1 tablespoon yellow mustard
- 1 tablespoon vinegar
- ⅛ teaspoon paprika
- French fries, for serving.

Directions:

Start by making the honey mustard sauce. Combine all the ingredients in a bowl, whisk, and set it in the refrigerator until you are ready.

Place the chicken breast strips in a resealable bag.

In a mixing bowl, combine the egg, buttermilk, and garlic powder and stir to combine. Pour this mixture over the chicken in the bag, and refrigerate for at least 2 hours.

In another large bag or shallow dish, combine the flour, bread crumbs, salt, and baking powder.

After the chicken has marinated, remove it from the refrigerator. Discard the extra buttermilk mixture.

Place the chicken pieces one or two at a time into the flour and bread crumb bag. Shake the bag to coat the chicken thoroughly.

Heat the oil in a large skillet to 375°F and carefully place the chicken in the hot oil. Cook until the outside is golden-brown, and the chicken is cooked through.

Place the pieces on a paper towel-lined plate to drain.

Serve with honey mustard sauce and French fries.

Nutrition: Calories 1375 kcal Protein: 47.05 g Fat: 42 g Carbohydrates: 205.41 g

Fiesta Lime Chicken

Preparation time: 10 minutes
Cooking time: 20 minutes
Serving: 4
Ingredients:

- 4 boneless skinless chicken breasts
- 2 tablespoons olive oil
- Salt and pepper to taste
- ¼ cup ranch dressing
- ¼ cup Greek yogurt
- 1 tablespoon lime juice
- ¼ cup fresh cilantro chopped
- 1 clove garlic, minced
- ½ cup Colby cheese, shredded
- ½ cup Monterey jack cheese, shredded
- For serving
- Mexican Rice
- Pico de Gallo
- Tortilla strips

Directions:
Preheat the grill or the oven to 400°F.
Brush the chicken breasts with olive oil, then season with salt and pepper as desired.

Grill the chicken for about 10 minutes on each side, or bake for 20 minutes in the oven, until it is cooked through and the juices run clear.
In a mixing bowl, combine the ranch dressing, yogurt, lime juice, cilantro, and garlic. Stir well.
Just before the chicken is done, spread a bit of the dressing mixture over each breast and top with a portion of the cheeses. Continue to cook until the cheese is melted.
To serve, plate a scoop of Mexican rice and place a chicken breast on top. Add Pico de Gallo and tortilla strips.
Nutrition: Calories 1244 kcal Protein: 44 g Fat: 103.86 g Carbohydrates: 36.31 g

Margherita Chicken

Preparation time: 20 minutes
Cooking time: 25 minutes
Serving: 4
Ingredients:

- 4 boneless skinless chicken breasts
- Spice rub
- 2 tablespoons packed brown sugar
- Juice of 1 lime
- 1 tablespoon oil
- 2 tablespoons paprika
- 1 tablespoon chili powder
- 1 tablespoon ground cumin
- 1 ½ teaspoons salt
- 1 teaspoon pepper
- Glaze
- ½ cup ketchup
- ¼ cup balsamic vinegar
- 1 teaspoon oregano
- ¼ cup packed brown sugar
- Cheese topping
- 1 cup mozzarella cheese, shredded
- ½ cup Parmesan cheese, grated
- Bruschetta

- 2 cloves garlic, chopped
- 2 teaspoons balsamic vinegar
- ½ teaspoon kosher salt
- ¼ teaspoon fresh cracked pepper
- 2 tablespoons chopped fresh basil
- 3 tablespoons olive oil
- 6 Roma tomatoes, diced

Directions:
Combine all the rub ingredients and spread the mixture over the chicken, using your fingers to massage it into the meat. Cover the chicken with wrap and refrigerate for at least an hour.

When the chicken is almost done marinating, make the bruschetta. Combine the garlic, vinegar, salt, pepper, and basil in a small bowl. Stir to combine. Slowly whisk in the olive oil, then add the tomatoes. Cover with plastic wrap and set aside until you are ready to assemble.

In a small bowl, mix all together with the glaze ingredients.

After your chicken has marinated, preheat the grill and set the oven to broil. Cook the chicken over medium-high heat until the juices run clear, and the meat has an internal temperature of 165°F. While the chicken is cooking, occasionally brush glaze over the breasts but watch them carefully so they don't burn.

When chicken is done on the grill, place it on a baking tray and top it with both the mozzarella and Parmesan cheeses. Set them below the broiler and cook until the cheese is melty and a bit bubbly.

Serve the chicken topped with the bruschetta topping.

Nutrition: Calories 1650 kcal Protein: 70.62 g Fat: 80.16 g Carbohydrates: 180.9 g

Shrimp and Parmesan Steak

Preparation time: 5 minutes
Cooking time: 20 minutes
Serving: 2
Ingredients:

- 1 cup heavy cream
- ½ cup Parmesan cheese, grated
- 2 teaspoons dried basil
- Salt and pepper to taste
- 2 (8 ounces) ribeye steaks
- 8 ounces shrimp (or prawns), peeled, deveined, and tails removed
- 1 tablespoon butter, melted

Directions:
Preheat your grill. You can cook these on the stovetop, but the smoky flavor added to the dish by grilling brings the best flavor.
Over medium-low heat, put the heavy cream to a simmer in a saucepan After you have reached a simmer, stir in the cheese and basil and season with salt and pepper. Lower the heat to remain the sauce warm while you cook the shrimp and the steak.

Spice the steaks with salt and pepper (or whatever spices you like on your meat). Grill for about 4 minutes on each side or to your desired doneness.

Cook the shrimp on the grill for about 40 seconds to a minute on each side, basting with melted butter.

To serve, put a steak on each serving plate. Top with grilled shrimp and a scoop of the Parmesan sauce.

Nutrition: Calories 1987 kcal Protein: 167.64 g Fat: 135.9 g Carbohydrates: 23.95 g

Mesa Grill's Crusted Filet Mignon

Preparation time: 20minutes
Cooking time: 8 minutes
Serving: 4
Ingredients:

- Roasted Red Pepper and Ancho Salsa
- 2 ancho chiles
- ½ cup boiling water
- 4 cloves garlic, chopped
- 2 tablespoons pine nuts
- 1 tablespoon honey
- 2 roasted red bell peppers, stripped
- 2 tablespoons red wine vinegar
- 3 tablespoons cut fresh cilantro leaves
- ½ teaspoon salt
- ¼ teaspoon ground black pepper
- For the Steak
- 4 (8-ounce) filet mignon steaks
- 1 tablespoon vegetable oil
- ½ teaspoon salt
- 4 teaspoons black pepper, coarsely
- 8 ounces fresh goat cheese, cut into 4 slices
- Cilantro leaves, for garnish

Directions:

Prepare the salsa. Pour the boiling water over the ancho chilies and let it sit for 1 hour. Remove the chilies from the water (keep the water) and chop the chilies, discarding the stems and seeds. Place them in a blender with ¼ cup of the soaking liquid, the garlic, pine nuts, and honey. Process until smooth. In a medium bowl, combine the purée with the bell peppers, red wine vinegar, cilantro, salt, and pepper. Cover the bowl and keep it at room temperature for 1 hour, or up to 4 hours. Heat the grill to medium-high. Clean and oil the grates. Brush the steaks with oil. Sprinkle both sides with salt and press the peppercorns into one side of each steak. When the grill is hot, cook the steaks pepper side down for about 3 minutes, until the pepper is nicely charred. Turn over the steaks and cook them another 4 minutes or so on the other side (for medium-rare, internal temperature measures 135°F). In the final minute of cooking, place a slice of cheese on top of each steak, and allow it to melt a bit. Rest the steak for 5–10 minutes before serving. Plate each steak and top with the Red Pepper Ancho salsa.

Nutrition: Calories 3465 kcal Protein: 244.75 g Fat: 246.71 g Carbohydrates: 58.81 g

Texas Roadhouse's Red Chili

Preparation time: 20 minutes
Cooking time: 1 hour
Serving: 6
Ingredients:

- 2 tablespoons vegetable oil
- 2 pounds beef chuck, cut into bite-sized cubes
- 1 yellow onion, diced
- 2 cloves garlic, chopped
- 1 ½ teaspoon chili powder
- 1 teaspoon ground cumin
- 1 teaspoon paprika
- 1 teaspoon salt
- ½ teaspoon black pepper
- ¼ teaspoon red pepper flakes
- 1 tablespoon brown sugar
- 1 ½ cups crushed tomatoes
- 2 teaspoons white vinegar
- 1 (15-ounce) can red kidney beans
- 2 jalapeños, seeded and sliced
- Optional for topping
- Shredded cheddar
- Green onions, chopped

Directions:
Heat the oil and cook the meat well in a saucepan.

Add the onion and cook to soften, and then stir in the garlic and cook until fragrant.

Add the chili powder, cumin, paprika, salt, pepper, red pepper flakes, and brown sugar. Mix to combine.

Stir in the crushed tomatoes and vinegar. Set the pot to a simmer, cover, and cook for 30 minutes.

Add the kidney beans and jalapeños and cook 10 more minutes.

Serve hot with a sprinkle of shredded cheese and green onion.

Nutrition: Calories 2335 kcal Protein: 232.49 g Fat: 139.91 g Carbohydrates: 43.17 g

Chili's Baby Back Ribs

Preparation time: 15 minutes
Cooking time: 3 hours and 30 minutes
Serving: 4
Ingredients:

- Pork
- 4 racks baby-back pork ribs
- Sauce
- 1½ cups water
- 1 cup white vinegar
- ½ cup tomato paste
- 1 tablespoon yellow mustard
- ⅔ cup dark brown sugar packed
- 1 teaspoon hickory flavored liquid smoke
- 1½ teaspoons salt
- ½ teaspoon onion powder
- ¼ teaspoon garlic powder
- ¼ teaspoon paprika

Directions:
Mix all of the sauce ingredients and then bring to a boil.
When the sauce starts to boil, reduce it to a simmer. Continue simmering the mixture for 45 to 60 minutes, mixing occasionally.
When the sauce is almost done, preheat the oven to 300°F.

Choose a flat surface and lay some aluminum foil over it to cover 1 rack of ribs. Place the ribs on top.

Remove the sauce from heat and start brushing it all over the ribs. When the rack is completely covered, wrap it with the aluminum foil and place it on the baking pan with the foil's opening facing upwards. Repeat steps 3 to 5 for the remaining racks.

Bake the ribs for 2½ hours.

When they are almost done baking, preheat your grill to medium heat. Grill both sides of each rack for 4 to 8 minutes. When you are almost done grilling, brush some more sauce over each side and grill for a few more minutes. Make sure that the sauce doesn't burn.

Transfer the racks to a large plate and serve with extra sauce.

Nutrition: Calories 1635 kcal Protein: 176.65 g Fat: 52.42 g Carbohydrates: 98.55 g

New York Strip

Preparation time: 5 minutes
Cooking time: 15 minutes
Serving: 4
Ingredients:
1 ½" steak (about ¾ lb.)
Salt and black pepper, to taste
2 teaspoons of olive oil
4 garlic cloves, in skins
1 sprig of fresh rosemary
Directions:
Set the oven's temperature to exactly 425° F;
Heat a medium cast-iron skillet over medium-high heat;
Season the steak with ½ teaspoon of salt and pepper;
Add the oil to the pan, add the steak, garlic, and rosemary and cook until the steak is golden brown, about 3 minutes per side;
Move the pan to the broiler and bake until the steak is at the desired point, 3 to 6 minutes over medium heat;
Move the steak to a cutting table and let it rest for at least 5 minutes before slicing.

Nutrition: Calories 198 kcal Protein: 7.84 g Fat: 15.27 g Carbohydrates: 8.43 g

Skillet Rib Eye Steaks

Preparation time: 30 minutes
Cooking time: 25 minutes
Serving: 4
Ingredients:

- 2 (1 ¼ lb.) bone-in steaks on the rib
- 2 tablespoons of Stone House seasoning
- 4 tablespoons of fresh rosemary leaves, chopped
- 2 tablespoons of butter, unsalted
- 2 tablespoons of olive oil

Directions:
Set the rib steak on the baking sheet and rub both sides with Stone House seasoning to coat, squeezing the seasoning well into the meat. Sprinkle with fresh rosemary leaves;
Carefully cover and refrigerate your rib-eye steaks for up to 3 days;
When you are ready to cook your rib-eye steaks, remove them from the refrigerator and let them sit and rest at room temperature for 30 minutes. Remember, if you are preparing your steaks to cook immediately, leave them at room temperature for 30 minutes;
To cook, heat a medium pan over medium heat. Add the butter and oil to the pan and let the butter melt completely;
Lean the pan from side to side to make sure it is coated with butter and oil;

Add the rib steak in butter and oil and cook until the bottom of the rib is brown and caramelized, about 5 minutes;

Turn the rib eye steak and cook, while basting the rib eye steak continuously with the butter and oil dripping from the pan, until this side of the rib eye steak is brown and caramelized, another 5 minutes or at the desired internal temperature for cooking;

Remove the rib eye steak from the heat and rest on a board for another 5 minutes;

Cut your steak with a sharp knife against the grain, taking care to remove the bone;

Set the slices of steak on two plates to serve.

Nutrition: Calories 2960 kcal Protein: 171.07 g Fat: 247.65 g Carbohydrates: 11.34 g

Filet Mignon

Preparation time: 10 minutes
Cooking time: 20 minutes
Serving: 4
Ingredients:

- 2 tablespoons extra virgin olive oil
- 4 (6 oz.) filet mignon
- Salt, to taste
- Black pepper, ground, to taste
- 4 tablespoons butter, softened
- 1 tablespoon rosemary, roughly chopped

Directions:

Leave the steaks sitting on the counter to reach room temperature for at least 30 minutes before cooking;

Preheat the oven to 400° F;

Lightly spray the steak with olive oil and season generously on both sides with salt and black pepper;

When the oven is ready, heat the pan over high heat until the pan is very hot;

When it is completely hot, add the steaks and cook, without stirring for 2½ minutes. Turn the other side and cook for another 2 to 2½ minutes;

Carefully cover the sides of the steaks for about 1 minute, so that they are browned everywhere;

Set the prepared steaks in the oven for about 4 to 5 minutes and check them with the meat thermometer inserted in the side of the steak; Remove when steaks indicate 125° F for Medium Rare or 130° F for Medium;
Allow it to stand for 5 or 10 minutes before serving (the temperature of the meat will rise by 5 to 10° F after it comes out of the oven).
Nutrition: Calories 606 kcal Protein: 7.29 g Fat: 64.31 g Carbohydrates: 1.86 g

Dessert

Lemoncello Cream Torte

Preparation time: 15 minutes
Cooking time: 4-5 hours
Serving: 8-10
Ingredients:

- 1 box yellow cake mix
- Limoncello liqueur (optional)
- 1 package ladyfinger cookies
- 1 (3-ounce) package sugar-free lemon gelatin
- 1 cup boiling water
- 1 (8-ounce) package cream cheese, softened
- 1 teaspoon vanilla extract
- 1 (13-ounce) can cold milnot (evaporated milk), whipped
- For the glaze:
- 1 cup confectioner's sugar
- 1–2 tablespoons lemon juice

Directions:

Preheat the oven to 350°F.

Make the yellow cake mix based on the directions on the package. Use two 9-inch round cake pans, or you can use a springform pan and cut the cake in half after it is baked.

When the cake is ready and cooled, you can soak the layers lightly with some limoncello. Do the same with the ladyfingers.

Put one cup of water to a boil and stir in the lemon gelatin. Refrigerate until it gets thick, but don't let it set.

Mix the cream cheese and vanilla, then mix in the thickened gelatin. Fold the whipped milnot into the mixture until combined.

To assemble the cake, place the bottom layer of the cake back in the pan. This will help you get even coats. Top the cake with about half an inch of the lemon filling. Place ladyfingers on top of the filling, then top with another layer of the filling. Put half of the cake on the top. Place the cake in the refrigerator to set.

Make a drizzle with some lemon juice and confectioner's sugar, and drizzle over the cake.

Nutrition: Calories 1558 kcal Protein: 55.97 g Fat: 76.57 g Carbohydrates: 163.39 g

Oreo Cookie Cheesecake

Preparation time: 10 minutes plus 4–6 hours refrigeration time
Cooking time: 60 minutes
Serving: 8-10
Ingredients:

- 1 package Oreo cookies
- ⅓ cup unsalted butter, melted
- 3 (8-ounce) packages cream cheese
- ¾ cup granulated sugar
- 4 eggs
- 1 cup sour cream
- 1 teaspoon vanilla extract
- Whipped cream and additional cookies for garnish

Directions:
Preheat the oven to 350°F.

Crush most of the cookies (25-30) in a food processor or blender, and add the melted butter. Press the cookie into the bottom of a 9-inch springform pan and keep it in the refrigerator while preparing the filling.

In a mixing bowl, batter the cream cheese until smooth and add the sugar. Beat in the eggs in one a time. When the eggs are mixed, beat in the sour cream and vanilla.

Chop the remaining cookies and fold them gently into the filling mixture.

Pour the filling into the springform pan and bake at 350°F for 50–60 minutes. Ensure the center of the cake has set.

Let the cake cool for 15 minutes, then carefully remove the sides of the springform pan. Transfer to the refrigerator and refrigerate for 4–6 hours or overnight.

Nutrition: Calories 3765 kcal Protein: 104.51 g Fat: 317.94 g Carbohydrates: 129.47 g

Banana Cream Cheesecake

Preparation time: 20 minutes
Cooking time: 1 hour and 30 minutes
Serving: 4
Ingredients:

- 20 vanilla sandwich cookies
- ¼ cup margarine, melted
- 3 (8-ounce) packages cream cheese, softened
- ⅔ cup granulated sugar
- 2 tablespoons cornstarch
- 3 eggs
- ¾ cup mashed bananas
- ½ cup whipping cream
- 2 teaspoons vanilla extract

Directions:
Preheat the oven to 350°F.
Crush the cookies in either a food processor or blender. When they have turned to crumbs, add the melted butter. Place the mixture in a springform pan and press to entirely cover the bottom and up the sides of the pan. Refrigerate this while you prepare the filling.

Batter the cream cheese until it is smooth, and add the sugar and corn starch. When the cheese mixture is well blended, add in the eggs one at a time.

When the eggs are incorporated, add the bananas, whipping cream, and vanilla, beating until well combined.

Place the filling into the springform pan and bake at 350°F for 15 minutes. Reduce the heat to 200°F and bake until the center of the cheesecake is set, about 1 hour and 15 minutes.

When the center is set, remove the cake from the oven. Pop the spring on the pan, but don't remove the sides until the cheesecake has cooled completely. When it is cool, transfer it to the refrigerator. Refrigerate for at least 4 hours before serving.

Serve with whipped cream and freshly sliced bananas.

Nutrition: Calories 4648 kcal Protein: 97.47 g Fat: 334.47 g Carbohydrates: 325.34 g

Blackout Cake

Preparation time: 30 minutes
Cooking time: 35-45 minutes
Serving: 8-10
Ingredients:

- For the Cake:
- 1 cup butter, softened
- 4 cups of sugar
- 4 large eggs
- 4 teaspoons vanilla extract, divided
- 6 ounces unsweetened chocolate, melted
- 4 cups flour
- 4 teaspoons baking soda
- ½ teaspoon salt
- 1 cup buttermilk
- 1 ¾ cups boiling water
- For the Chocolate Ganache:
- 12 ounces semisweet chocolate, chips or chopped
- 3 cups heavy cream
- 4 tablespoons butter, chopped
- 2 teaspoons vanilla
- 1 ½ cups roasted almonds, crushed (for garnish)

Directions:

Preheat the oven to 350°F. Make-ready two large rimmed baking sheets with parchment paper (or grease and dust with flour 3 8-inch cake pans).

In a large bowl or bowl for a stand mixer, beat together the butter and sugar until well combined. When the sugar mixture is fluffy, add the eggs and 2 teaspoons of vanilla. When that is combined, add the 4 ounces of melted chocolate and mix well.

In a separate bowl, stir together the flour, baking soda, and salt. Gradually add half the flour mixture to the chocolate mixture. When it is combined, add half of the buttermilk and mix until combined. Repeat with remaining flour mixture and buttermilk. When it is completely combined, add the boiling water and mix thoroughly. (The batter should be a little thin).

Divide the batter evenly between the two large baking sheets that you prepared earlier (or 3 8-inch cake pans).

Take to the oven and bake for 20–30 minutes for the baking sheets or 25-35 minutes for the cake pans, or until a toothpick inserted in the center comes out clean.

Remove from the oven and let cakes cool for about 10 minutes. With the pastry ring, make 3 cakes from each of the baking sheets. When they are completely cool down. If using cake pans, turn them out onto a cooling rack and cool completely and then cut horizontally into two to make 6 cake layers

Make the ganache by mixing the chocolate chips and cream in a heat-safe glass bowl. Bring the bowl over a pot of boiling water. Reduce heat to medium-low and let simmer gently. Blend constantly with a wooden spoon until the chocolate is all melted. Add-in the butter and vanilla and stir until well combined. Let cool for a few minutes, cover with plastic wrap, and refrigerate until the ganache holds its shape and is spreadable about 10 minutes.

To assemble the cake, place the first cake layer on a serving plate and spread some of the ganache on the top. Set the second cake layer on top and covered some of the ganache on top. Repeat until all 6 layers are done. Use the excess ganache to frost the top and sides of the cake, then cover the sides with crushed almonds (if desired) by pressing them gently into the chocolate ganache. Refrigerate before serving.

Nutrition: Calories 9799 kcal Protein: 125.91 g Fat: 410.88 g Carbohydrates: 1395.99 g

S'mores Layer Cake

Preparation time: 45 minutes Cooking time: 8-10 minutes
Serving: 10
Ingredients:

- Graham cracker layer
- 3 cups graham cracker crumbs
- 1 cup butter, melted
- Chocolate fudge layer
- 3 cups chocolate chips
- 2½ cups condensed milk
- Marshmallow layer
- 3 packets gelatin
- ¾ cup of warm water
- 3 7-ounce containers marshmallow fluff
- Chocolate ganache
- ¾ cup heavy cream
- 1 cup of chocolate chips
- Garnish
- Marshmallow fluff
- Mini-marshmallows
- Graham cracker crumbs & chunks
- Chocolate chunks

Directions:

The simplest way to ensure this cake comes out of the pan nicely is to line your springform pan with parchment at both the bottom and the sides. Then spray with nonstick cooking spray.

Blend the graham cracker crumbs and melted butter together in a mixing bowl. Press about ⅓ of the mixture into the bottom of the pan. In a separate bowl, combine the chocolate chips and condensed milk. Microwave at 2-minute intervals until the chocolate melts. Stir until smooth.

Pour ⅓ of this mixture over the top of the graham cracker crumbs in the springform pan.

Dissolve 1 packet of gelatin in ¼ cup of warm water. When completely dissolved, mix the gelatin with one jar of marshmallow fluff and stir until smooth. Spread the marshmallow mixture evenly over the top of the crumbs and chocolate in the springform pan.

Put the pan in the refrigerator for 5–10 minutes to set. Then remove from the fridge and repeat the layers: crumbs, chocolate, and another packet of gelatin mixed with fluff. You will make 3 layers in total, refrigerating in between to ensure the layers remain separate. Refrigerate overnight.

Before you are ready to serve, make the chocolate ganache by heating the heavy cream in the microwave for 3 minutes or until it starts to simmer lightly. Then pour it over the chocolate chips in a bowl. Mix until smooth, then let cool to room temperature.

Take the cake out of the refrigerator, remove the parchment paper, and place it on a serving plate. Pour the chocolate over the cake. It's okay if it sprinkles down the sides; it adds flavor on its way down. Top with marshmallow fluff, toasted graham chunks, and chocolate chunks. Serve.

Nutrition: Calories 11542 kcal Protein: 63.67 g Fat: 862.21 g Carbohydrates: 920.06 g

Zeppole

Preparation time: 20 minutes
Cooking time: 15 minutes
Serving: 12
Ingredients:

- 1 (¼-ounce) package active dry yeast
- 1 cup water (divided)
- 1½ cups all-purpose flour
- 1-quart vegetable oil (for frying)
- 2 tablespoons confectioners' sugar
- Chocolate sauce for dipping

Directions:
In a pot, heat oil to 375°F.
Let the yeast dissolve in ½ cup of warm water for 10 minutes. Stir the remaining water into the bowl.
Add the flour and combine until a dough form.
Knead on a smooth surface, then place into a greased bowl. Turn to coat the dough. Place a damp cloth on top to cover.
Let the dough rise for 1–1½ hours in a warm room. Cut and roll into golf-ball-sized pieces.

Fry until golden brown. Drain on top of a paper towel. Sprinkle with confectioners' sugar. Serve with chocolate sauce on the side.
Nutrition: Calories: 827 kcal Protein: 25.77 g Fat: 7.9 g Carbohydrates: 159.04 g

El Chico's Deep-Fried Ice Cream

Preparation time: 10 minutes
Cooking time: 2 minutes
Serving: 4-6
Ingredients:

- 1 cup Corn Flakes® crumbs
- ½ cup of sugar
- ½ teaspoon cinnamon
- 1-quart vanilla ice cream
- For serving
- Chocolate or caramel syrup (or both)
- Whipped cream
- Maraschino cherries
- Oil for frying

Directions:
Combine the crushed cereal crumbs with the sugar and cinnamon in a shallow bowl.
Set out a baking dish or pan.
Allow the ice cream to soften slightly. Scoop out balls and roll them in the coating mixture.
Set them on the prepared pan and return them to the freezer for 5 hours.
Heat the oil to 450°F. Working quickly and one at a time, lower the ice cream balls into the oil. Cook for 2 or 3 seconds only, and remove them to a serving dish.

Top with whipped cream, syrup, and a cherry, and serve!
Nutrition: Calories 611 kcal Protein: 13.06 g Fat: 6.44 g
Carbohydrates: 127.3 g

Abuelo's Sopapillas

Preparation time: 30 minutes
Cooking time: 15 minutes
Serving: 8
Ingredients:

- 1 ⅓ cups all-purpose flour
- 1 teaspoon baking powder
- ¼ teaspoon salt
- 1 ½ tablespoons shortening
- ½ cup lukewarm water
- Oil for frying
- Cinnamon sugar for dusting

Directions:
Combine the dough ingredients and mix gently until a dough form. Let the dough sit for 30 minutes.
Meanwhile, heat the oil to 375°F.
Roll out the dough ¼-inch thick (or thinner) and cut it into squares.
Fry until golden brown on both sides.
Drain the sopapillas on a sheet of paper towel and dust with cinnamon sugar while they are still warm.
Serve immediately.
Nutrition: Calories 857 kcal Protein: 23.58 g Fat: 26.89 g
Carbohydrates: 126.9 g

Chili's Paradise Pie

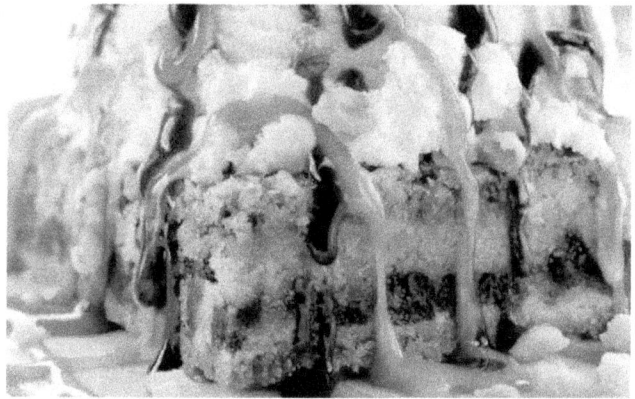

Preparation time: 15 minutes
Cooking time: 20 minutes
Serving: 24
Ingredients:

- 3 cups flour
- 1 teaspoon baking powder
- ½ cup (1 stick) butter, at room temperature (softened)
- 3 cups brown sugar, packed
- 6 eggs
- 3 teaspoons vanilla
- 1 cup shredded coconut
- 2 cups milk chocolate chips
- 1 cup chopped walnuts, plus more for sprinkling
- Topping
- Vanilla ice cream
- Caramel sauce, for drizzling
- Chocolate or hot fudge sauce, for drizzling

Directions:
Preheat oven to 325°F. Grease a half-size sheet or 2 rectangular pans.
Strain flour and baking powder together in a bowl. Set aside.
Cream the butter with an electric mixer.
Add the sugar to incorporate.
Put the eggs one at a time, beating continuously at medium speed.
Add vanilla.
Add the flour mixture and mix to incorporate.

Add coconut, chocolate, and walnuts, mixing briefly to distribute unto batter.

Transfer to prepared saucepan.

Bake until a toothpick press in the center comes out clean (about 40 minutes).

Let cool slightly until easy to handle.

Serve hot, topped with vanilla ice cream and drizzled with caramel and chocolate sauces.

Nutrition: Calories 5059 kcal Protein: 122.77 g Fat: 222.19 g Carbohydrates: 646.37 g

IHOP Cinn-A-Stacks

Preparation time: 20 minutes
Cooking time: 20 minutes
Serving: 4
Cinnamon Sauce Ingredients:

- 1 tablespoon of all-purpose flour
- ⅛ teaspoon of ground cloves
- ⅛ teaspoon of sea salt
- 1 tablespoon of ground cinnamon
- 3 tablespoons of half-and-half cream
- ¾ cup of dark brown sugar
- ¼ cup of salted butter
- Cream Cheese Icing Ingredients:
- ¼ teaspoon of vanilla extract
- 1 teaspoon of lemon juice
- 1 ¼ cups of powdered sugar
- 4 ounces of softened cream cheese

Garnish:
Whipped cream
Directions:
Over medium heat, place a tiny pan and melt the butter in it. Add the salt, cloves, cinnamon, 2 tablespoons of half-and-half cream, and brown sugar and continue to cook while continually stirring until the mixture simmers. Take the sauce off the heat, add the remaining half-and-half cream and flour, and continue to stir until blended.

Use a medium bowl and an electric mixer to prepare the cream cheese icing. Mix these ingredients over low speed until you get a smooth mixture. Fill a squirt bottle with this mixture.

Spread some cinnamon sauce on top of each pancake. IHOP usually serves two pancakes on top of each other, but it's up to you to decide how many of you want. I recommend you stick with 2—spread cream cheese icing on the stack. Don't forget to add whipped cream on top.

Nutrition: Calories 1461 kcal Protein: 10.64 g Fat: 63.89 g Carbohydrates: 220.18 g

IHOP Country Griddle Cakes

Preparation time: 5 minutes
Cooking time: 10 minutes
Serving: 8-10
Ingredients:

- 2 teaspoons of salt
- ¼ cup of vegetable oil
- 1 teaspoon of baking soda
- 1 teaspoon of baking powder
- ⅓ cup of granulated sugar
- 1 egg
- ⅓ cup of instant Cream of Wheat (dry)
- 1 ½ cups of buttermilk
- 1 ¼ cups of all-purpose flour
- Nonstick spray

Direction:
Take a frying pan, coat the surface of it with nonstick spray, and place it over medium heat.
Use a large bowl to mix all the ingredients using an electric mixer on medium speed. Blend until you get a smooth mixture.
Take portions of ⅓ cup of batter and put them in the pan—Cook the pancakes between 1 to 3 minutes (or until the base turns golden brown). Flip to cook on the other side for about the same amount of time, or until it turns golden brown. Repeat the process for the remaining batter. Serve warm.
Tip: These go well with maple syrup.

Nutrition: Calories 1603 kcal Protein: 44.94 g Fat: 78.34 g Carbohydrates: 181.01 g

IHOP Funnel Cakes

Preparation time: 10 minutes
Cooking time: 30 minutes
Serving: 14
Ingredients:

- 2 to 3 cups of vegetable oil
- ½ teaspoon of baking powder
- 2 cups of all-purpose flour
- ½ teaspoon of salt
- 1 teaspoon of vanilla extract
- 1 ¼ cups of whole milk
- ⅔ cups of granulated sugar
- 3 eggs
- Toppings
- Whipped cream
- 3 ½ cups blueberry, strawberry, or cinnamon-apple pie filling
- Powdered sugar

Directions:

Use a bowl and an electric mixer to whisk the eggs and sugar on medium speed. Pour in some milk, add the vanilla and salt, and continue to blend until the sugar has dissolved.

In another bowl, blend the flour with baking powder, and then drop them into the wet ones. Use the electric mixer to mix them all over medium speed, cover the mixture, and let it cool for about an hour.

Over medium heat, heat the oil in a saucepan. Prepare the funnel by spraying it with nonstick spray and pour portions of ¼ cup of batter into it. It takes about one minute for the dough to turn golden brown on the bottom, then you can flip it over to cook it on the other side as well. Each funnel cake has to be removed to a paper towel to drain, and covered with foil to keep warm.

Serve each funnel cake with powdered sugar and about ½ cup of filling of your choice, and add whipped cream on top for a unique taste.

Tip: To remove any bubbles from the batter, tap on the side of the funnel. It should take practice to master the art of making funnel cakes since the way you pour the mixture determines if the funnel is too thin or too thick. The funnel has to be kept close to the oil, not in it. When you pour the batter, make sure you go from one end of the funnel to another. I prefer doing the movements from up to down and then from left to right. Pour the batter steadily, not too fast or too slow.

Nutrition: Calories 6477 kcal Protein: 74.02 g Fat: 485.77 g Carbohydrates: 499.4 g

Applebee's Chocolate Mousse Dessert Shooter

Preparation time: 10 minutes
Cooking time: 20 minutes
Serving: 4
Ingredients:

- Canned whipped cream
- ½ cup of chocolate fudge sauce
- 8 Oreo cookies
- ½ cup of heavy cream
- 2 tablespoons of brown sugar
- 2 eggs, separated
- 1 teaspoon of vanilla extract
- 1 tablespoon of Godiva Chocolate Liqueur
- 6 ounces of semisweet chocolate chips (or 1 cup)
- 2 tablespoons of salted butter

Directions:

Prepare a double boiler by placing a metal bowl inside a medium skillet over low heat. Fill the skillet with a couple of inches of water, and let it heat while you put a piece of butter in the metal bowl. After the butter has melted, you can add the chocolate chips, leaving at least 1 tablespoon of them aside. After the chocolate melts, add the vanilla and chocolate liqueur. Take the metal bowl out of the skillet and whisk in the egg yolks. Use a separate bowl to whisk the egg whites until you get soft peaks. Pour this mixture into the other mixture and stir. Use another medium bowl to mix sugar and cream. Whip the cream until it gets stiff. Add the whipped cream into the chocolate mixture. The remaining chocolate chips have to be chopped into small bits (the size of rice), stir them into the mousse and cover it for 3 to 4 hours to cool down. Empty the filling of the Oreos, place the chocolate cookies into a plastic bag and pound on it until you get a bag full of crumbs (you can use a kitchen mallet for this task). Use 6-ounce rock glasses for each serving. Spoon 2 tablespoons of Oreo crumbs into the bottom of each glass, add ⅓ cup of chilled mousse and top it off with two tablespoons of chocolate fudge. It's easier to heat the fudge into the microwave first before spooning it into a glass. Add some whipped cream on top and some leftover Oreo crumbs.

Tip: You can also use off-brand chocolate cookies with white filling.

Nutrition: Calories 2703 kcal Protein: 39.95 g Fat: 140.69 g Carbohydrates: 320.86 g

Applebee's Key Lime Pie Dessert Shooter

Preparation time: 10 minutes
Cooking time: 20 minutes
Serving: 4

- Key Lime Filling Ingredients
- ½ cup of key lime juice
- 14 ounces of condensed milk
- 4 egg yolks
- Key Lime Topping Ingredients:
- Canned whipped cream
- ½ cup plus 2 teaspoons of graham cracker crumbs
- 3 tablespoons of powdered sugar
- 2 teaspoons of key lime juice
- ½ cup of sour cream

Directions:

Use a medium bowl and an electric mixer to beat the egg yolks on high speed for about 2 to 3 minutes or light yellow. Add the condensed milk and mix for 30 more seconds. Pour the mixture into a medium pan that was placed over medium-low heat, and stir in ½ cup of key lime juice. Cook for 8 to 10 minutes and stir very often, until you notice the mixture starting to bubble. Remove over the heat and let it cool for about 3 to 4 hours.

Prepare the key lime topping by mixing key lime juice, powdered sugar, and sour cream. Cover the topping and let it cool.

For each serving, prepare a 6-ounce rock glass, spoon 2 tablespoons of graham cracker crumbs into it, add ½ cup of key lime filling, and add 2 tablespoons of topping on top.

Add whipped cream on top, sprinkle about ½ teaspoon of crumbs on it, and enjoy.

Tip: If you choose to use fresh key limes, one lime provides about 2 tablespoons of juice.

Nutrition: Calories 798 kcal Protein: 28.73 g Fat: 44.16 g Carbohydrates: 77.8 g

Applebee's Strawberry Cheesecake Dessert Shooter

Preparation time: 10 minutes
Cooking time: 20 minutes
Serving: 4
Cheesecake Filling Ingredients:

- ½ teaspoon of vanilla extract
- 2 tablespoons of sour cream
- ⅓ cup of granulated brown sugar

- 2 eggs, beaten
- 12 ounces of cream cheese

Garnish:
- Canned whipped cream
- ½ cup of frozen sliced strawberries in syrup,
- ½ cup of graham cracker crumbs

Directions:
Use a large bowl to prepare the cheesecake filling by mixing the sugar, cream cheese, eggs, sour cream, and vanilla extract. Use a mixer on high speed for this job, and blend until smooth. Place a large saucepan over medium-high heat, and pour the mixture in it. Prepare the mixture for about 8 to 10 minutes by continually stirring until the mixture thickens. When ready, the mixture should stick to the spoon. Pour the mixture into a container, cover it, and let it cool for several hours. For each serving, use a 6-ounce rock glass. Put 2 tablespoons of graham cracker crumbs in the bottom, and on top, add ⅓ cup of cheesecake filling. Finish each serving by adding syrup and 2 tablespoons of strawberries. Serve with whipped cream on top of the dessert.

Tip: An electric mixer works best, but you can also mix it by hand.

Nutrition: Calories 1617 kcal Protein: 43.57 g Fat: 119.93 g Carbohydrates: 94.81 g

Salted Caramel Skillet Cookie

Preparation time: 10 minutes
Cooking time: 40 minutes
Serving: 4
Ingredients:

- 1 cup of butter, room temperature
- ½ cup sugar, granulated
- 1 cup of light brown sugar
- 2 large eggs
- 2 tablespoon vanilla essence
- 2 tablespoon milk
- 2 ½ cups flour, all-purpose
- 1 teaspoon cornstarch
- 1 teaspoon baking soda
- ½ teaspoon salt, or to taste
- 1 cup semi-sweet chocolate chips
- 20 caramel squares
- 1 chocolate candy bar, broken into pieces
- 2 teaspoons salt

Directions:
Set the oven's temperature to exactly 325° F;
Lightly grease oven-safe, 10" cast iron skillet (you have to make use of a safe oven skillet);

Beat the butter smooth and creamy in mixer bowl with a paddle attachment;

Add both the brown and sugar, granulated then beat on medium-high until fluffy and light;

Beat in eggs, milk, and vanilla on the speed that is high until well mixed;

Scrape down the sides and the bottom part of the bowl as needed if not making use of a scraper paddle attachment;

Add flour, cornstarch, baking soda as well as salt on low speed until combined;

Add the chocolate chips and mix on low;

Transfer ½ the cookie dough into prepared skillet and press down into an even layer;

Add ½ the chocolate bar, caramel parts, and ocean salt;

Top with remaining dough, pressing down then and again with a remaining chocolate candy bar, salt, and caramel;

Bake for nearly 27 to 30 minutes or until browned on the sides and lightly brown on top. In case you love it a bit more cooked through, bake for exactly 35 to 40 minutes;

Let the cookie cool slightly in the pan on a wire rack before serving.

Nutrition: Calories 4360 kcal Protein: 52.15 g Fat: 216.69 g Carbohydrates: 547.8 g

Cranberry Bliss Bar: Starbucks Copycat

Preparation time: 10 minutes
Cooking time:
50 minutes
Serving: 3 dozen
Ingredients:

- .75 cup Cubed butter
- 1.5 cups Light brown sugar - packed tight
- 2Unchilled large eggs
- pinch Cinnamon
- 2.25 cups all-purpose flour
- .25 tsp. Salt
- 1.5 tsp. Baking powder
- .5 cup Dried cranberries
- .75 tsp. Vanilla extract
- 6 oz. Coarsely chopped white baking chocolate

The Frosting:

- 8 oz. pkg. Unchilled cream cheese
- 1 cup Confectioner's sugar
- 6 oz. Melted white baking chocolate

- .5 cup Chopped dried cranberries
- 1 tbsp. Optional: Grated orange zest
- Also Needed: 13x9-inch pan

Directions:
Set the oven to reach 350° Fahrenheit.

Melt the butter in a large bowl, mixing in the brown sugar. Cool the mixture for a minute or two.

Whisk and add in one egg at a time, and add the vanilla.

Whisk the cinnamon, baking powder, flour, and salt. Stir it into butter mixture. Fold in the berries and chocolate. Spread the thick batter into a greased baking pan.

Bake it until golden brown (18 to 21 min.). Don't overbake. Cool on a wire rack.

Prepare the frosting. Mix the confectioners' sugar, cream cheese, and orange zest until it's creamy. Slowly mix in half of the melted white chocolate, spreading it over the blondies.

Sprinkle with the berries and rest of the melted chocolate.

Cut it into triangles. Place them in an airtight dish in the fridge.

Nutrition: Calories 220 kcal Protein: 4.75 g Fat: 16.56 g Carbohydrates: 12.86 g

Fudge Brownies: Saxby's Copycat

Preparation time: 15 minutes
Cooking time: 30 minutes
Servings: 12
Ingredients:

- 1 stick/.5 cup Butter
- 2 Oz. Semi-sweet dark chocolate
- .75 cup Sugar
- .5 cup Unsweetened cocoa powder
- 1.5 tsp. Vanilla
- 3 Eggs
- .5 cup All-purpose flour
- 1 tsp. Baking powder
- .75 tsp. Salt
- .5 cup Optional: Walnuts
- Also Needed: 8" x 8" baking pan

Directions:
Set the oven to reach 350° Fahrenheit. Chop the nuts and chocolate. In a pan, melt the butter and chocolate using the low-temperature setting on the stovetop. Stir in the cocoa, sugar, and vanilla and remove the pan from the heat.

Whisk and add in the baking powder, eggs, flour, and salt. Whisk the batter until smooth and stir in the walnuts.

Pour the batter into the baking tray coated with a bit of nonstick cooking oil spray.

Spread the batter out and bake it for 20 to 25 minutes. If you like your brownies less fudgy, bake it for a few extra minutes.

Nutrition: Calories: 254 kcal Protein: 15.73 g Fat: 18.36 g Carbohydrates: 5.83 g

Harvest Pumpkin Frozen Yogurt: Menchie's Copycat

Preparation time: 10 minutes
Cooking time: 30 minutes plus freezing 1-2 hours
Serving: 8
Ingredients:

- 1 quart Frozen - softened - fat-free vanilla yogurt
- .5 cup canned pumpkin
- .3 cup Packed brown sugar
- .75 tsp. Pumpkin pie spice
- .25 cup Toasted - chopped pecans

Directions:
Combine all of the fixings except for the pecans.
Place in a freezer container and chill until solid.
Sprinkle with the nuts when served.
Nutrition: Calories 835 kcal Protein: 16.4 g Fat: 84.51 g
Carbohydrates: 15.11 g

Hershey's S'mores Cookies: Pizza Hut Copycat

Preparation time: 10 minutes
Cooking time: 20 minutes
Serving: 16
Ingredients:

- .5 cup shortening
- .5 cup Sugar
- .5 cup Peanut butter
- .5 cup Packed brown sugar
- 2 Unchilled large eggs
- 1.5 cups + 5 tbsp. All-purpose flour
- .5 tsp. Vanilla extract
- 1 cup/6 oz. Semisweet chocolate chips
- 2 cups Miniature marshmallows
- Also Needed: 12-inch pizza pan

Directions:
Set and preheat the oven at 375° Fahrenheit.
Cream the peanut butter, shortening, and sugars until they're fluffy.
Mix in the eggs and vanilla. Lastly, mix in the flour.
Pat the mixture into a greased pan. Bake it for 16 minutes.
Sprinkle it using the chocolate chips and marshmallows. Bake it until lightly browned (3-5 min.).
Nutrition: Calories 29816 kcal Protein: 1170.93 g Fat: 1216.92 g
Carbohydrates: 3547.09 g

Timeless Restaurant Favorites

Starbucks® Mocha Frappuccino

Preparation time: 10 minutes
Cooking time: 10 minutes
Servings: 8
Ingredients:

- ¾ cup chocolate syrup
- 4 cups of milk
- ¾ cup of sugar
- 3 cups espresso coffee

For Topping:

1. Chocolate syrup
2. Whipped cream

Directions:

Prepare the coffee as per the directions provided by the manufacturer. Mix hot coffee & sugar in a mixer until the sugar is completely dissolved, for a minute or two, on high settings.

Add chocolate syrup & milk; continue to mix for a minute more.
For easy storage, pour the mixture into a sealable container. Store in a refrigerator until ready to use.
Now, combine mix & ice (in equal proportion) in a blender & blend until smooth, on high settings & prepare the drink.
Pour the drink into separate glasses & top each glass first with the whipped cream & then drizzle chocolate syrup on the top.
Serve & enjoy!
Nutrition: Calories: 197 kcal Protein: 4.54 g Fat: 4.47 g Carbohydrates: 35 g

Reese's Peanut Butter Cups

Preparation time: 15 minutes
Cooking time: 2 minutes
Chill time: 6 hours
Servings: 10
Ingredients:

- Salt, pinch
- 1½ cups peanut butter
- 1 cup confectioners' sugar
- 20 ounces milk chocolate chips

Directions:
Take a medium bowl and mix the salt, peanut butter, and sugar until firm.
Place the chocolate chips in a microwave-safe bowl and microwave for 2 minutes to melt.
Grease the muffin tin with oil spray and spoon some of the melted chocolate into each muffin cup.
Take a spoon and draw the chocolate up to the edges of the muffin cups until all sides are coated.
Cool in the refrigerator for 1 or 2 hours (or until it cool).

Once the chocolate is solid, spread about 1 teaspoon of peanut butter onto each cup.

Leave space to fill the edges of the cups.

Create the final layer by pouring melted chocolate on top of each muffin cup.

Let sit at room temperature until cool.

Refrigerate for a few hours until firm.

Remove the cups from the muffin tray and serve.

Nutrition: Calories 455 Total fat 21.7 g Carbs 59 g Protein 9.7 g Sodium 384 mg

Cadbury Cream Egg

Preparation time: 15 minutes
Cooking time: 2 minutes + Chill time: 3 hours 30 minutes
Servings: 6
Ingredients:

- ⅓ cup light corn syrup
- ⅓ cup butter
- 2 teaspoons vanilla
- ⅓ teaspoon salt
- 3½ cups white sugar, ground and sifted
- 3 drops yellow food coloring
- 2 drops red food coloring
- 16 ounces chocolate chips, milk
- 3 teaspoons vegetable shortening

Directions:
Take a bowl and combine corn syrup, butter, vanilla, salt, and powdered sugar.
Mix all the ingredients well with a beater.
Reserve ⅓ of the mixture in a separate bowl, then add food coloring.
Chill both portions in the refrigerator for 2 hours.
Form rolls from the orange filling, about ¾-inch in diameter.
Wrap the orange rolls with white filling.

Repeat until all of the mixtures are consumed.
Form in the shape of eggs.
Let sit in the refrigerator for 1 hour.
Melt the chocolate chips in the microwave.
Dip each egg roll in the melted chocolate.
Cool in the refrigerator for 30 minutes.
Once solid, serve, and enjoy.
Nutrition: Calories 1004 Total fat 34.8 g Carbs 174 g Protein 5.9 g Sodium 261 mg

Hot n' Spicy Buffalo Wings from Hooters

Preparation time: 10 minutes
Cooking time: 10 minutes
Servings: 4
Ingredients:

- Vegetable oil, for deep frying
- ¼ cup flour
- 1¼ teaspoons Cajun seasoning, divided
- ¼ teaspoon oregano
- ¼ teaspoon basil
- ⅛ teaspoon cayenne pepper
- Kosher salt
- 2 cups dill pickles, drained and sliced
- ¼ cup mayonnaise
- 1 tablespoon horseradish
- 1 tablespoon ketchup

Directions:
Preheat about 1½ inches oil to 375°F in a large pot.
In a separate bowl, make the coating by combining flour, 1 teaspoon
Cajun seasoning, oregano, basil, cayenne pepper, and Kosher salt.
Dredge pickle slices in flour mixture. Lightly shake to remove any
excess, then carefully lower into the hot oil. Work in batches so as not
to overcrowd the pot. Deep fry for about 2 minutes or until lightly
brown.
Using a slotted spoon, transfer pickles to a plate lined with paper
towels to drain.

While pickles drain and cool, add mayonnaise, horseradish, ketchup, and remaining Cajun seasoning in a bowl. Mix well.

Serve immediately with dip on the side.

Nutrition: Calories 296 Total fat 28 g Saturated fat 14 g Carbs 12 g Sugar 4 g Fibers 0 g Protein 1 g Sodium 1201 mg

Deep-Fried Pickles from Texas Roadhouse

Preparation time: 10 minutes
Cooking time: 10 minutes
Servings: 4
Ingredients: Vegetable oil, for profound broiling

- ¼ container flour
- 1¼ teaspoons Cajun flavoring, separated
- ¼ teaspoon oregano
- ¼ teaspoon basil
- ⅛ teaspoon cayenne pepper Kosher
- salt two mugs dill pickles, depleted and cut
- ¼ glass mayonnaise
- 1 tablespoon horseradish
- 1 tablespoon ketchup

Directions:

Preheat almost 1½ inches oil to 375°F in an expansive pot.
 In a separate bowl, make the coating by combining flour, 1 teaspoon
Cajun flavoring, oregano, basil, cayenne pepper, and Legitimate salt.
Dredge pickle cuts in the flour blend. Softly shake to expel any
abundance, at that point carefully lower into the hot oil. Work in
clumps so as not to stuff the pot. Deep sear for approximately 2
minutes or until softly brown.
Using an opened spoon, exchange pickles to a plate lined with paper
towels to deplete.

While pickles deplete and cool, include mayonnaise, horseradish, ketchup, and remaining Cajun flavoring in a bowl. Blend well. Serve quickly with a plunge on the side.

Nutrition: Calories 296 Total fat 28 g Saturated fat 14 g Carbs 12 g Sugar 4 g Fibers 0 g Protein 1 g Sodium 1201 mg

Avocado Eggrolls from The Cheesecake Factory

Preparation time: 15 minutes
Cooking time: 5 minutes
Servings: 8
Ingredients:

- Cilantro dipping sauce
- ¾ cup fresh cilantro leaves, chopped
- ⅓ cup sour cream
- 2 tablespoons mayonnaise
- 1 garlic clove
- 2 tablespoons lime juice
- Salt and pepper, to taste
- Egg roll:
- 1 cup vegetable oil
- 3 avocados, peeled and seeded
- 1 Roma tomato, minced
- ¼ cup red onion, minced
- 2 tablespoons fresh cilantro leaves, diced
- 2 tablespoons lime juice
- Salt and pepper, to taste
- 8 egg roll wrappers

Directions:

Mix the ingredients for the cilantro dipping sauce in a bowl. Set aside.
Preheat a large pot with oil over medium-high heat. Oil temperature
should reach 350°F and there should be enough oil to cover the rolls,
about 3 to 4 inches deep Mash avocados in a bowl. Mix in tomato, red
onion, cilantro, and lime juice. Add salt and pepper, to taste.
Position avocado mixture onto the middle of an egg roll wrapper. Fold
wrapper on top of mixture and roll until the mixture is fully wrapped—
secure edges of the wrapper by pressing with water using your finger.
Repeat for the remaining mixture and wrappers.
Deep-fry rolls in the pot of hot oil for at least 2 minutes or until all
sides are golden brown.
Remove from pot with tongs and place onto a plate lined with paper
towels.

Serve with the cilantro dipping sauce on the side.

Nutrition: Calories 288 Total Fat 18 g Carbs 28 g Protein 6 g Sodium 219 mg

Copycat Bloomin' Onion and Chili Sauce from Outback

Preparation time: 20 minutes
Cooking time: 4 minutes
Servings: 8
Ingredients:

- 2 huge sweet onions such as a Vidalia
- Oil for frying
- Seasoned flour:
- 1 container flour
- 2 teaspoons paprika
- 1 teaspoons garlic powder
- ¼ teaspoon pepper
- ⅛ teaspoon cayenne
- Chili sauce (yields 2 ¼ mugs):
- 1 container mayonnaise
- 1 mugs acrid cream
- ¼ container tomato chili sauce
- ¼ teaspoon cayenne

Dipping Sauce:

- ½ glass mayonnaise
- 2 teaspoons ketchup
- 2 teaspoons horseradish cream
- ¼ teaspoon paprika

- ¼ teaspoon salt
- ⅛ teaspoon dried oregano
- 1 sprint dark pepper
- 1 sprint cayenne

Batter:
- ⅓ container cornstarch
- 1½ mugs flour
- 2 teaspoons garlic, minced
- 2 teaspoons paprika
- 1 teaspoon salt
- 1 teaspoon pepper
- 24 ounces brew

Directions:
Preheat a huge pot with oil over medium-high warm until 375 °F, not surpassing 400 °F.

In a huge bowl, blend the fixings for the prepared flour.

In a partitioned bowl, blend the fixings for the chili sauce.

For the plunging sauce, blend the fixings in a bowl and keep refrigerated. To make the batter, put together cornstarch, flour, garlic, paprika, salt, and pepper in a bowl. Blend well.

Pour in the brew to the bowl of dry fixings. Mix continuously until smooth.

Chop into ¾ inches of the onion on the top. At that point, Peel cut until fair over the foot root conclusion to create approximately 14 vertical wedges. Remove about 1 inch of petals from the interior.

Coat petals in flour, at that point, shake off any excess—dip in a batter. Make beyond any doubt the onion is well-coated.

Deep-fry for almost 1 to 3 minutes, or until brilliant brown. Move onto a plate with paper towels to drain.

Serve with chili sauce and plunging sauce on the side.

Nutrition: Calories 404 Total Fat 12 g Carbs 59 g Protein 8 g Sodium 436 mg

The Famous Breadsticks from Olive Garden

Preparation time: 15 minutes
Cooking time: 15 minutes
Servings: 16
Ingredients:

- 1½ cups plus 2 tablespoons warm water
- 1 package active dry yeast
- 4¼ cups all-purpose flour
- 2 tablespoons unsalted butter, softened
- 2 tablespoons sugar
- 1 tablespoon fine salt
- 3 tablespoons unsalted butter, melted
- ½ teaspoon kosher salt
- ¼ teaspoon garlic powder
- Pinch dried oregano

Directions:
Preheat oven to 400°F. Provide a baking tray and line it with parchment paper.

To prepare the dough, pour ¼ cup warm water in a mixing bowl. Add yeast and wait 5 minutes or until bubbles form. Combine with flour, 2 tablespoons butter, sugar, salt, and 1¼ cups and 2 tablespoons warm water. Mix for about 5 minutes or until mixture turns into dough that is a bit sticky. Remove from bowl and transfer onto a flat surface sprinkled with flour.

Moistened for about 3 minutes until dough is soft and smooth—form dough into a log that is about 2 feet long. Then, cut dough equally in 1½-inch long pieces, making 16 small pieces in total. For each piece, knead slightly and form into a breadstick that is about 7 inches long—position breadsticks on the prepared baking tray with 2-inch spaces between each. Cover, then set aside for 45 minutes or until dough size has doubled.

Using a brush, coat breadsticks with 1½ tablespoons melted butter—season with ¼ teaspoon salt.

Place in oven and bake for 15 minutes or until slightly golden.

As the breadsticks bake, mix remaining salt, garlic powder, and oregano in a bowl.

Remove breadsticks from the oven and immediately coat with the rest of the melted butter—season with herb mixture.

Serve warm.

Nutrition: Calories 146 Total fat 4 g Saturated fat 2 g Carbs 25 g Sugar 2 g Fibers 1 g Protein 4 g Sodium 456 mg

Conclusion

Copycat recipes have become very popular with the ever-high cost of eating out. Secret recipes from all your favorite restaurants can prepare them for the comfort of your home.

The most significant advantage of using copycat restaurant recipes is that you can save money, but, if needed, you can customize the recipes. For example, if you want to reduce the salt or butter in one of the plates, you can. Now you've saved money, and at the same time providing a nutritious meal for your family.

You have little control over the ingredients in the meal when you eat out. You can't adjust the dish that you order because sauces, etc. are made in advance.

We all know it is expensive to take the family out for dinner, and without a doubt, you can quickly drop a hundred dollars on the table. With copycat restaurant recipes, the same one hundred dollars can promptly produce four or more meals.

Now, imagine having all the necessary ingredients at home for a second to cook the same dish with a copycat restaurant. So when you're making a copycat restaurant recipe, you can "wow" your family and guests.

You're going to have them thinking you've picked up dinner from a favorite restaurant just by using these recipes and saving costs compared to dining out.

Trying to guess what the ingredients are to your favorite restaurant meal is eliminated when you use copycat recipes. You follow the recipes and slowly recreate your favorite meal.

Having regular meals inspired by your favorite restaurants as a family allows for a healthier, more tight-knit family. Research has shown that in school, families who dine together at home are more united, happier, and the kids perform better.

To sum up, the huge savings you'll gain from cooking at home could be used for more productive things like a family holiday or college tuition for your kids.

Going out for a meal at your favorite restaurant is always fun to most. But what if you had access to the top-secret restaurant recipes that so heavily guard those popular restaurants? Would you go home cooking these yourself whenever you wish?

It is not that difficult to learn how to cooktop secret restaurant recipes. Some think you need a degree in culinary arts or cooking education to cook those secret recipes. I hate telling you this, but anyone can collect the ingredients and cook a fancy meal that tastes like the real thing.
But do top secret restaurant recipes taste the way the chef served them? Perhaps. You can quickly cook your favorite recipes with a little practice and patience.
The advantage of making your own top-secret is that you can add your flavors and spices to your recipes. You'd want to cook the basic formula and start adding what you think would make the recipe's flavor better after a while.
Cooking top secret recipes from restaurants will make your friends and family wonder where you've learned to cook so well. Imagine cooking a whole meal that looks like it was the restaurant's take-out food. I bet some friends of yours won't even believe you've cooked it!

CPSIA information can be obtained
at www.ICGtesting.com
Printed in the USA
BVHW072123100321
602204BV00011B/592